Valedictory Verses

A. G. PRYS-JONES

GOMER PRESS
1978

First Impression — 1978

ISBN 0 85088 840 9

© A. G. PRYS-JONES

PRINTED BY J. D. LEWIS AND SONS LTD.,
GOMER PRESS — LLANDYSUL

FOREWORD

ANYONE rash enough, like myself, to offer the public another volume of poems at the age of 90, would certainly be well-advised to describe it as "Valedictory Verses". Though the human heart is credited with vast reservoirs of hope, the extension of terrestrial leaseholds to nonagenarians isn't usually lavishly granted. In my own case, however, another volume gives me the opportunity of expressing my sincere gratitude to the appreciative group of people who have found some interest and enjoyment in the kind of verse I produce, and to those who have also found pieces of mine suitable for verse-speaking in schools and elsewhere. So, to them I am happy to dedicate this final book.

Of the 40 poems included herein, 24 have not hitherto appeared in personal volume form, though many have been printed in modern anthologies, and in the *Anglo -Welsh Review, Poetry Wales, Country Quest* and elsewhere. Two Welsh lyrics have been brought in from the old *Y Llenor* via a previous volume, with four short pieces taken more or less intact from the latter source. But with the itch for "improving" early efforts which afflicts some poets, I have re-written, lengthened or otherwise altered 8 pieces from volumes long out-of-print, all perhaps with satisfaction only to myself !

I cannot conclude without extending my warmest thanks to my old friends Hugh Bevan, Dr. Glyn Jones and Elwyn Evans for their generous practical advice and encouragement at all times, and to a valued new friend, Don Dale-Jones, who keeps me in touch with Dyfed, and who has bravely undertaken to steer this volume through the Press after delays on my part which would have exhausted the patience of a saint.

Diolch o galon i chi oll.

A. G. PRYS-JONES

CONTENTS

GRANDFATHER CLOCK

I CUT the tiny throats of seconds
And stun the minutes at their birth,
Garotte the hours with groan and shudder,
Wheezing my mild Herodian mirth.

This house and I, grown old together,
Have seen the decades ebb and flow,
And watched your kinsmen's infant faces
Age and wither : and fade and go.

What irony that one whose cloister
Is but a corner in your hall
Is now the block, the mask of black,
The headsman and the axe that wait you all.

THE VETERAN

*(An old soldier who had served in the Second Afghan War,
1878—1880)*

BESIDE his cottage in warm, sunny days
He slept in snatches, wrapped in memories.
But sometimes after sundown he would wake
Alertly from his rambling reveries,
And tell of stirring times to eager boys
Who listened, waiting in the quiet cool
Of eventide, for every vivid word
Of his swift march with Roberts to Kabul.
And so, held spell-bound by the veteran
Of frontier battles, sieges, ambuscades,
We heard across the Clwydian hills and glades
Loud echoes of high tumults from afar,
The frenzied drums of fierce Afghanistan,
The thunder of the guns of Kandahar.

YOUNG GIRL

(From the Welsh of "Geneth Ifanc" by Waldo Williams)

A budding girl once graced this stony skeleton,
And every time anew she holds me in thrall ;
For each year of my age I go back a century
To bring her kith and kin within recall.

Her people trod the paths of peacefulness,
Buying the bounties of earth with skill and wit ;
They pondered the mystery of birth and marriage and dying,
And kept the frail bonds of humanity knit.

Crouched in her early grave she was buried,
A dozen times she had seen the blossom of May
When the dark fellow-traveller took her,
And her voice on the uplands faded away.

Deeper then were the sky's blue spaces,
Bluer than blue because of her presence there,
More steadfast the timeless, invisible dwelling
Abiding for her on this hill-top bare.

(Skeleton in the Avebury Museum from an early settlement on nearby Windmill Hill. Probable date about 2,500 B.C.)

ON MYNYDD HIRAETHOG

(For Berwyn, Helen and Gail)

HIGH in a marshy hollow
On heather-hued Hiraethog
There stands marooned for ever
So it seems,
A massive monolith
Aborted from a melting glacier's womb
In ages long ago
When these great moorlands lay
In bondage to harsh dynasties of ice.

Now, here it looms
A stark, forbidding stone
Gigantic in the mists of early morning :
And riven from its kin,
Remote and solitary, deaf and mute,
Bereft of all authority,
It cannot hear
The credulous, croaking frogs
Who pledge their hoarse allegiances
Around the plashy feet
Of their imagined monarch.

It cannot see
The questing, hovering kestrel
Contracting to a speck
Before its plummet-swoop
On unsuspecting prey :
Or watch the calm, unhurried fox
Loping at ease to his lair
Beneath the dark dome
Of the pines.

Immune to all disease, immovable
Save by some huge catastrophe
Contrived by evil men,
Or by a freak
Of pitiless, unheeding nature,
It draws no breath, is warmed
By no one. Desolate and doomed
To endless solitude, it cannot feel
The fires of love, the poignant pain
And spear-thrusts of bereavement.
Alone through endless days
Of blind monotony,
It can never reach
The haven of old age,
Nor wait with calm assurance
To grasp the gentle, kindly hands
Of healing, all-revealing death.

RETURN

Faint echoes of far distant bells
In summer woodlands where I lay
Awoke long buried memories,
When once before I passed this way
To lives ahead.

A wandering poet, harp-struck, fey,
Cast out from some Cistercian cell
Because the youthful vows I made
Had not been grafted on too well,
The Abbot said.

There was another with me then,
Of what strange birth is past surmise,
But with her here, this hidden glade
Became a transient paradise,
And our green bed.

Perchance in other sojournings
On earth or realms one knows not where,
I still may find in ardent quest
The singing dryad who was there
And loved and fled.

SILVER BOY

Who is this silver boy
That I should fear to meet
His merry face, and hear
His flying feet
Wake memories in the mornings
Of the street ?

For eighty years
The hidden mirror ran
Concealed within the sun and rain
That sped the springing wheat,
Reflecting all the changes
In the man :
While I the captive
Of an unknown plan
Had never looked therein
Nor wondered at the garments
That the decades spin.
And now, in what remote retreat
Dwell those successive images of mine,
The vanished legion I have been ?

If in some secret festival
We could assemble, each and all,
To recreate with magic skill
Of Math and Gwydion
That early face of glowing joy,
Would he accuse us
Of betrayal,
That silver boy ?

TAKEOVER PARABLE

SEVEN princes all aspired to rule a kingdom,
Because (they claimed) their king was old and daft :
These princes (and their wives) were so ambitious
They tried to wipe each other out by craft.
One vanished without trace, and two were poisoned,
The fourth was strangled, the fifth stabbed dead in bed,
The last two fought a duel and died wounded,
The old king then mopped up : the wives had fled.

Seven peasants in a hamlet in that kingdom
Had no ambitions but to win their bread,
Pay silly taxes, sleep, and do some loving,
And have a priest say Mass when they were dead :
They sometimes beat their wives, got drunk and roistered,
But, all in all, were honest, earthy folk,
And so they stayed alive while round about them
The dreams of their seven princes crashed and broke.

WHEN TIME DRIFTS DOWN

(In memory of the Welsh composer, Evan T. Davies)

WHEN time drifts down like falling autumn leaves
And lethargy, at last, has come to stay,
Then cock-crow's clarion wakes no citadel,
No towers are stormed by stealth at crack of day,
For old ambitions, fears and urgencies
Have loosened grip and lost their power to sway.

Along the stubbled fields the mists of evening
Enfold the threadbare wraiths that wander there,
Frail actors of the myths of memory,
Pale simulacra of the dreams that were.

Here are the borders, almost intertwined,
Of two terrains, the one explored and charted,
The other's frontiers still to probe and find,
Yet open to awareness, and then faintly spied
At times, through curtains suddenly parted,
By some kind sentinel on the other side.

And here the old, earth's winter-weary children,
Await the final crossing of the line,
Receiving first the solace of oblivion,
The gift of nature's gracious anodyne :
And then release, like snowflakes softly falling
In silent warmth along the frozen wold,
Until their opening eyes discern before them
The new dimensions wherein none grow old,
And hear the welcome of departed voices calling.

AQUARIUM

FLASHES of brilliant colour
Changefully moving,
Darting, twisting and turning
Vivaciously, joyously,
With superb and delicate skill
In this green, man-made image
Of a deep-sea garden.

Perfectly posed,
Miraculously fashioned,
Beautifully proportioned,
These tiny, elegant creatures
Are living jewels that glow,
Gleam and sparkle
In their watery element,
As if always conscious
Of the perpetual wonder
They awake in onlookers.

God be praised for His wisdom
In permitting prodigal nature
To lavish
Such exquisite beauty
Upon the small,
The defenceless and meek.

HIGH COMPANY

OVER the plains of dusk
My memories walk and roam
Like gleaners in a harvest-field
After the harvest-home :

Searching the stubbled years
Now winnowed of grief and pain,
For all the joys and ecstasies
That I would share again

With friends in my quiet room :
And there by the lilting fire
I open the doors of the dark
To the guests of my desire.

They gather in from the night,
They had never wholly fled,
And so I hold high company
With those I deemed long dead.

IN SNOWDONIA

(A hill-farmer poet speaks)

My heritage is in a high domain,
A place of princely hawks, the royal breed
Of Gwynedd's ancient dynasty :
And when I sought its solitudes again
Among these austere mountains of my youth,
Their towers unprofaned and still untaken,
In one swift touch of intuition
Revealed along the vast serenity
Of massy hills, ravines and forest glens,
I knew a sick world well forsaken
For sanctuary in this eyrie of Eryri.

And here in the cold clop and cling
Of winter's brassy feet, through minstrel spring
And summer's flirt of roses, to the dying fall
Of autumn's russet faith, I hold dominion
From the loud sheep-fold to the wild terrain
Where curlews make their plaintive, whistling call,
And plovers wander restless before rain :
While down the steep of granite stone
My deep black pearl, the silent, brooding tarn,
On lustrous nights seems lit for me alone.

And so I live in sane content
Working the primal crafts of words and soil :
And often when my speeding days are spent,
And nights are clear and windless, after toil
I stand to praise the high, celestial art
Of stars that turn their myriad notes of fire

To music in the glittering galaxy,
And from the lowly station of my heart
Salute their endless symphony.

At times, from cliff-tops I can hear
The cadences of waves in depths below,
Those children of the moon, attuned to moods
Of their bright mother in their ebb and flow :
Like springtide trees and autumn woods
That quicken pulses and make sharp the breath,
They build and break their blossomed crests
Renewing strength and beauty after every death.

And thus I know reality
Lies not within the compass of our clay,
For though our bodies at the journey's end
Are mute as unhewn marble and as cold,
The vibrant self, freed from its transient mould
Of circumscribed awareness, will fare forth,
Shedding the shackles of both time and space,
To richer, more abundant realms of being,
For after mortal midnight dawns immortal day.

Though I am old and lean upon my spade
(So often now before I rise and go),
I glimpse with awe and wonder,
In meditation upon all things made,
Creation's ultimate design for man.
My scanty wisdom tells me this is so,
For I have seen great darkness fail and fade.

VIROCONIUM

THE hated Saxon hosts swooped down to ravage,
The Yellow Plague came killing from the East :
And now the granaries heaped high with harvest
Hold not a grain for famished man or beast.

No watchman waits upon the tumbling turret,
No sentinel walks along the crumbling wall :
Nothing is left that any man could covet,
No maid, no chattel—nor an ox in stall.

Charred beams lie burnt and broken in the market,
Forsaken hearths are cold and dumb in dust,
The toppled temples filled with fallen rubble,
The marbles crusted with the rain's red rust.

Here nothing stirs, the dead lie deep in silence
Where murrain strides the grey, miasmal ground,
Until at last a withered host awakens
To march towards the hills without a sound.

(*Wroxeter on the Severn, Roman fortress and tribal centre of the British Cornovii, sacked by the invading Saxons.*)

SALT MARSHES

THESE marsh-lands evoke sorrow
And bring fear,
For I can feel
The ancient grief of grass, the gloom of water,
And sense the lurking terror
Which haunts the landscape here,
The menace of those potent, unseen powers
That ride their wings of dread to hag the dark :
See how that witch, the twilight, hastening near
Makes sharp her sickle-edge to mow the day,
And how the ragged mendicants of mist
Rise up in shrouded garb from stealthy lairs,
Thrusting their shapeless hands around one's face
Obtruding, clammy, obdurate and clinging.

The sun has set, the tide creeps trembling in
Muting its rhythmic cadences :
The black dykes gurgle, like small children choking,
In quick convulsions, speechless and afraid :
And the grey flock of frightened sheep
Moves in a huddled mob to shelter.

This is no place for mortals,
It is anguished ground, and maybe Cain-accursed
Through violent deeds of darkness long ago :
Boorish and barren in its eldritch days
And pagan in its vows of vengeful evil,
Unhallowed grave for sea-men's flotsam bones
Picked white by plucking seas,
And sepulchre of shreds of winnowed ships
That once wove heraldry upon the waves
In full-sailed beauty, free from silting sands.

Yet I was comforted when I discerned
The blessed candle of a gentle spirit,
Like a white nun within a lazar house,
Drawn to this shore by some strong cord of love ;
And knew, with her oblations made and ended,
Redemption pouring in on shriven tides.

A DAY WHICH ENDURES NOT

(Adapted from the Welsh of Elidr Sais, 13th century poet)

As for me
I have seen Llywelyn
With all the valiant men of Wales around him,
His armies like the hosts of Merfyn ;
And have marched with chieftains mustering
On the steep hills and the deep lowlands,
Pillars of war were they all, and mighty.

I have seen brave youth in battle
And heard the high thunder of horsemen :
I have drunk rare wines from chalices,
With rich meats laid on fine linen
In the bountiful palaces of princes.

I have listened to golden oratory,
To the jewelled harmonies of bards
Declaiming their poems in intricate metres ;
I have heard the songs and satires
Of wandering minstrels,
And shared the merriment of maidens
Tickled by the saucy tales of story-tellers.

I have also known the thrill
Of great festivals and ceremonies,
The glamour and glitter of contests,
With the strong rejoicing in their prowess,
And the clever in their cunning.

But now all these have gone
Like dreams in the morning :
And so, each soul must journey forth
In the time of his reckoning
From a day which endures not.
In this the lord of many lands
The poor man's master
Gains no reprieve, no respite,
He passes through death's portals
With the peasant.

PILGRIM

HERE, at the cliff's sheer edge,
Watching the vast expanse
Of unpredictable waters,
Weary at last and bewildered,
I knew I had travelled far
Without sure sign or token,
Though always seeking and hoping.

Perhaps this was not the right way,
Not the true path at all :
There had been no voice
From the burning bush on the hill,
And I found no fiery prophet
Proclaiming his gospel
Along the reedy river beds
Of the baptising plains :
There were no holy anchorites
Hugging their private illuminations
Closely to their withered bodies
In the dank caves
Of the limestone coast,
To mutter even shadowy directions :
While that alluring jade,
The fickle sea,
Gave only contrary reflections.

Maybe I had still to wander
Further in harsh landscapes,
Over high, precipitous places,
Through the gloom of dark forests

And the desolate, sand-bound places
Of heat-stricken deserts,
Before glimpsing the oases of truth
With their welling fountains of wisdom.

For truth and wisdom are revealed
Only to the humble, seeking heart
With self clean-winnowed :
Then, often unexpectedly,
In sudden silence,
They blossom like a flame
In a timeless moment of knowing.

I had travelled a long way
Without sure sign or token,
But in the last
Clear shaft of sunshine on that day
Falling in radiance on the western hills,
I saw a bright rising of towers,
A brilliance of high places,
And heard a far murmur of wings :
The Kingdom shone there in its glory,
And I saw it,
The distant land and the promise,
In that certain, swift token of light.

AUTUMN STORM, GLAMORGAN COAST

THE wild sea hurls its ancient anger
Against the stubborn ramparts of the shore,
Like some vain Emperor whose monstrous pride
Demands new conquests, launching host on host
In thunder at the long-beleaguered land.

There is no plunder here, the tired trees
Have signalled their surrender to the winds,
The sea's fierce allies, sweeping through the groves
With whirling sabres, seeking autumn gold.
From ransacked treasuries they toss and fling
The coloured coinage madcap to the sky,
Like roaring, drunken, reckless prodigals
Not caring where their lavish largesse falls.

And I in my enforced neutrality,
Anonymous amid anarchic elements,
A captive sheltered on the shuddering cliff-top,
Watch the stark struggle of stupendous forces
In that gigantic battle, while the waves
Burst impotent in fury overhead :
And hear above the tumult of their onslaught
The high, victorious voices of the winds
Shrieking their challenge to the heedless stars.

THE AGELESS CHRIST

THE Ageless Christ, in mystery
Endures the ordeal of re-birth
To face again the agony
And monstrous infamies of earth.

He knows the snares the fowler lays,
The evil lures of power and might,
The hatred that enslaves and slays,
The terror stalking in the night.

He hears the cries of the oppressed,
The poor, the hungry and the old,
The sick, the lonely, the distressed,
Despairing in a world grown cold.

In Him is found the secret place,
The fortress of enfolding wings
Where they may dwell in healing grace
With angels in their journeyings.

For He has seen through darkening years
His gospel flouted and defied,—
And comes again to share the tears,
The Cross of all the crucified.

GWALCHMAI'S BOAST

(Adapted from the Welsh of Gwalchmai ap Meilyr, court poet to Prince Owain Gwynedd, predominant ruler of Wales in the 12th century.)

Over the misty, eastern moorlands
The dawn comes early
As summer marches on in glowing weather :
Sweet in my ears
Is the babble of birds
In the bright, blue air of morning.

Gold is my gleaming corslet,
Bold my heart,
Before a host there is no lion braver,
No lightning like my onset.

By night I have kept strong vigil
Shielding the shallow fords
Of the sighing waters of Dygen Freiddin.
Very green is the virgin grass,
Crystal the river,
And the mounting song of the nightingale
Is an ode which has no ending.

And now, since early summer,
My heart is filled with memories
Of the gracious girl I love
And left bereft at Caerwys,
That gentle fawn whose lips
And speech gave me contentment.
So here I stand, the liege-man of my lord
And generous patron, Owain Gwynedd,
Ready to speed the foe to flight
Before my faithful sword.

IN EARLY SPRING

ALONG the dormant woods, the daffodils
Emblazoning deliverance from winter's prison
Marshal their golden companies :
And graciously in cloisters of the Vale
Those pure, white nuns the snowdrops
Proclaim the coming miracles of Spring.

Through high, blue veils of cloud
A sun-meshed lark exultantly
Pours down his misty magic on the hills
In pearls of rounded song,
And even the timid grass finds courage
In that triumphant celebration :
While in the long lane, a stripling thrush, alone,
Asserts his tribal right to turn to melody.

Soon, the brave exuberance of bud and leaf
Surging in patterned sunlight from the trees
Will break in bright, green billows at my door,
And gentle winds will lead in stately saraband
My shy and slender silver birches.

When dawn comes winging with delight of birds,
And all things join in joyful praise,
And all things glorify their Maker,
Then who am I to keep
My heart in wintry frost before the Lord ?

RAINFALL AFTER PROLONGED DROUGHT

THE reservoirs were empty, arid acres,
The wells bone-dry in their sepulchral depths,
The brooks had died along their stony courses,
And the parched roots of pines in mountain places
Had groped in vain
Deep in these iron hills for water,
Where withered grass, grown weak with waiting,
Trembled there to crumbling dust,

Now day by teeming day
Rain falls at last in urgent mercy,
And as the sky's dark veins pour down
Their warm, redemptive blood
Come promises of rich revival
In vibrant resurrection.
And soon, bright choral blossoms
With psalters of rejoicing
Will sing the distances
Between gold wheatfields and the Severn flood.

But no rain falls in quickening benison
On barren pastures of the hearts of men
Grown faithless, heedless, hard, undisciplined
Within a world which groans in travail,
Where greed and folly, tyranny, despair,
Injustice, fear, vile cruelty and terror
Spring up in dreadful harvest,
The bitter fruits of men's unhallowed husbandry.

33

O suffering multitudes, bewildered, restless,
Bereft of roots, misguided and betrayed,
Return, rebuild again the ruined strongholds
Of your abandoned sanctuaries,
Regain the healing peace and strength
Of your forgotten silences !

TO A WELSH MYSTIC

Your eyes inspire : they draw their clear convictions
From sources which lie deeper than we know :
No storm, no deluge can engulf you,
No night of tempest which can make you quail.
You are serene and steadfast
Standing like a lighted house at nightfall
On a desolate moor
With hope in all its windows
For the forspent traveller.
Death is your friend, a kindly one and knightly,
There is no terror in his tread,
His hands are warm with bearing
Your kinsfolk gently through the portals.

You have seen beyond the barriers
The new realm, the place of many mansions :
You have seen the havens of healing
Where those blind with misunderstanding
Gain sight : they are like little, battered ships
Resting in quiet waters
Waiting to voyage onward.

Nobility shines in your countenance,
Humility reigns in your heart,
The gifts of love and laughter,
Happiness and humour are your heritage :
Your hands bring respite from pain,
Your words, solace in sorrow,
And your presence
Gives peace to the troubled and tormented :

Long may you abide
In the faith which is your fountain of strength,
And in your dwelling place
Of the green pastures.

AN OLD, OLD MAN

HERE at the borderland,
Here where his journey ends,
Who can we recall for him
Of his forgotten friends ?

Mutely, motionless, he stares
Bemused into a fitful fire
Which stirs no spark of memory,
No flicker of desire.

Alone upon a darkened road,
Oblivious of time and place,
Nothing now remains for him
Not even his love's face.

ON HEARING A FRIEND PLAYING ONE OF
RACHMANINOFF'S PRELUDES

FRENZIED hands at the coffin-lid
Under the yew tree newly hid :
Will never the sexton run to hark
At the fearful sounds that sear the dark ?

O rend, wood, rend ! O rip, nails, rip !
Loose the hold of your cruel grip !
Are only the dead stirred there in the gloom
By the struggle within that sounding tomb ?

Stertorous breathing, muffled, thick,
Screams and groans that follow quick :
O God send someone down the street
Who'll know why the drums of the churchyard beat !

Are friends and neighbours fast asleep
That no one sees the fresh turf creep ?
Is the parson deaf in the parsonage
That he cannot hear the yew tree rage ?

But nobody heard the muted knell
Of ghostly hands at the passing bell :
And whether he died with a curse or a prayer
None will know of his agony there.

Silent beneath the coffin-lid
Under the yew tree newly hid,
What does it matter now he's dead
That he died in his grave instead of his bed ?

THE PLOUGHMAN AND THE POET

(After Iolo Morganwg's invention of a poem by Dafydd ap Gwilym)

FROM dawn to early dusk
Plodding on, he drives his plough,
His hands pliant, his heart playful :
Sometimes he pulls aside, pausing for leisure,
Leaving his long, straight lines and sending
A blithe song to the blue sky,
Or lightening with gay lilting
His tawny oxen's toil.

Cunningly he fashions his clean furrows
From red woodland to round water :
The brown soil brings him solace,
In turned-up turf he sees his trove
Abundant in the joy of July's bounty,
The gold crops growing tall along the tilth.

I, too, the poet, ply my craft with pleasure,
But plough and sow for rarer harvest-yield,
With merry songs for Meirion's loving maidens
And golden odes for Gwynedd's aureate girls :
O my Morfudd of old magic, my Dyddgu,
Dark-haired, desirous ; my Gwen of adorable grace,
My generous Gwenonwy, my sibyl, my votaress !
To you, sighing, I send my sonnets
By swan or linnet, sea-gull or the lark,
Or by the minstrel wind in amorous mood :
And while, anxiously, I await answer,
I scatter largesse in rich rhymes of love.

VALE OF GLAMORGAN

Here the rapacious Norman came
To conquer and abide :
He wrought in stern, enduring stone
The symbols of his pride.

Turret and tower and rounded arch
Above the southern strand
Bear witness to his vanished might
In this enchanted land.

Close by his crumbled Priory walls
This golden autumn day,
A ploughman on once feudal fields
Goes his unchanging way,

Turning the ancient earth anew,
The soil that links them still,
The Norman in his tumbled tomb,
The Welshman on the hill.

AT THE GRAVE OF TWO WELSH PEASANTS WHO DIED IN 1795. THEIR TWELVE CHILDREN ALL EMIGRATED AND PROSPERED

THEIR mountain home, long derelict, has crumbled,
Their hard-won realm merged in the conquering waste,
Where only melancholy stones reveal
That here was once a happy dwelling-place
Loud with the merriment of tumbling children.
The parents' dust lies mingled with the soil,
The stubborn earth which bore reluctant bread
And gave the simple sustenance
Of peasants pinned to homesteads in harsh hills.

They had no time to quarrel over creeds,
No learning to dispute theologies :
Theirs was a simple faith which knew no doubt
That God's will worked in His mysterious ways
Ordaining always what was meet for them :
And so, immortal longings plagued them not,
While random happenings of time and chance
Were quietly accepted : these disturbed
No rhythm in each season's patient toil.
Secure within their kinsfolk's loyalties
And certain of their succour in duress,
They envied no one, bore no grudge or malice,
Kept close to ancient virtues, and then died,
Believing, in the end, all would be well.

These two believed not vainly, they have reached
Afar to lands known only in their dreams :
Their dozen stalwart sons and comely daughters
Inheriting their parents' skill and courage
And their strong faith, went forth, forsaking

These windy uplands where unceasing toil
Could furnish few rewards, and sailed abroad
One after one to prosper in their prime.
They cleared wild scrub and forest, made their settlements,
Built homes and chapels, raised new families
Who turned the fruitless earth to fields of grain,
And filled great spaces with their thundering herds.
Their pioneering grandsons and descendants
Tamed further deserts, won more frontiers,
Made room for townships, embryo cities,
Built railways, bridged deep gorges, tunnelled mountains,
And helped to found new states where none had been,
Sank pits, sought metals and made furnaces,
Established industries and built safe harbours
Where sturdy ships with food and merchandise
Set hard their helms for home.

Pause therefore at this lonely grave
And praise the lowly dust of two
Who by the alchemies of time and fate
Transmuted into gold in youthful lands
Their leaden days of sacrifice and striving.

GWLADUS DDU

(From the Welsh of G. J. Williams)

A white-robed chronicler took pen and wrote
On yellow parchment these brief words I quote
From annals of the Princes and the Blest,
"In that year Gwladus Ddu was laid to rest."

What moved the monk in that Cistercian vale
To mention her in his romantic tale ?
Did he attain his heaven at life's close
By seeing dawn beyond her dark repose ?

And I remembered in the warmth of home
With all Eryri's slopes as white as foam,
Seven hundred winters' snows had fallen there
Since summer glistened in her glossy hair.

As I perused that mellow script tonight
I glimpsed a shrunken face, once gay and bright,
Embalmed among the boldest and the best,
"In that year Gwladus Ddu was laid to rest."

(Gwladus Ddu was one of six children born to Llywelyn
the Great and his wife Joan, a natural daughter of King
John. Gwladus died in 1251. She was twice married, first
to Reginald de Breos and later to Ralph Mortimer, both
influential Norman marcher lords.)

YSTRAD FFLUR

(From the Welsh of T. Gwynn Jones)

THE swaying leaves at Ystrad Fflur
Murmur in myriad number
Where twelve white abbots, long at rest,
Lie deep in peaceful slumber.

Here, too, lies Dafydd, prince of song,
His yew grown old in grieving,
Near sword-bright chiefs whose annals all
Have gone beyond retrieving.

When summer wakes the woods to wear
Their hues of celebration,
Man does not wake, and all his works
Pass silent to oblivion.

Though sad, effacing death I see
Where faith lies devastated,
Yet when I walk at Ystrad Fflur
My anguish is abated.

THE COCK

(From the Welsh of Harri Gwynn)

THE cock crows
Stretching his neck,
With a trumpet-blast
Which tears the early dawn
Asunder.

He crows again,
And then descends to swagger
Among the flustered,
Newly wakened hens.

But we,
In out soft bed
And the tenderness of pillows,
Go drifting down again
Into the pit of sleep.

Soon,
He crows a third time,
And wakes us peevish,
Us, the betrayers.

ON HIS FAILURE TO CAPTURE A PRIZE AT SEA

*(Adapted from 'the quaint hodge-podge of good Welsh and poor
English' of Tomos Prys, Elizabethan soldier, poet and sometime
buccaneer.)*

> Over the water to Spain I went
> In an auspicious time, intent,
> If fortune favoured me at sea,
> On bringing back rich booty.
>
> "Mary be praised, I see a prize
> Sailing at ease before our eyes,
> Give chase grimly ere she goes
> Beyond our grasp, you hoboes !
> Turn topsail out, you tipsy lout,
> Get the wind, go all out !
> Gusty weather can do its worst,
> If we're brave we'll board her first.
> Fire again, a broadside, gunner,
> Another burst will stop and stun her :
> Fight for store and leave sorrow,
> Fear not, shoot the wildfire now :
> Lay her aboard, defy the din,
> Venture all and enter in."
>
> But in our struggle, hapless stroke,
> We lost good lads in the gun-smoke.
> "Give back lest all be taken !
> Are there no means to save more men ?"
> We found an unfortunate day
> And find we'll mind this Monday.
> We'd pluck in plenty but luck was lacking,

That prize which proved too strong for sacking,
No timid sheep for shearing,
Blazed back and struck our steering.
On wounded wings we crept away,
Sadly in spume of sea-spray.

"O Lord, this load's too hard to bear
With young Ffowc Harri drowning there,
Hit at the height of battle :
Brown Robin Austin, too, withal,
Is dead and so is Duddal,
Wenford, Rowland, and Winfield,
William and Cobham are all killed."

MOURNING A LONG-LOST LOVER

(From the Welsh of Tomos Prys, Elizabethan soldier, poet and sometime buccaneer.)

If my dead young darling still
Bides in her grave beneath the hill,
Dear Lord, I would long to lie there
Under her head to hold her hair.

If my Gwen below grey gravel
Still tarries in that same terrain,
A thousand leagues I'd swiftly travel
Through stormy stress of wind and rain,
So gladly without grief I'd go
To linger at her elbow.

If laid within her lonely mound,
She's captive, bound in oaken keeping,
I grieve that I'm not in the ground
Sharing her silvan sleeping.

If in that grave beside a grove
Fine soil falls on my girl's face,
Then, by Heaven, I'd dearly love
Soon to go, with God's good grace,
To be the guardian earth above
The placid place she lies therein,
Shielding her slender coffin.

A WINTER DAY

(Adapted from the Welsh of an unknown 11th century poet.)

CRUELLY falls the wind's flail
On wandering beast and wayfarer,
The white hill winnowed barren :
There is no shelter here, no shield
From the bitter blast
For weary men benighted.

The fords run high, the lake frozen,
Down there now, in furious hail,
A gasping man, forspent, could pause
To ease his wheezing breath
By leaning on a single rigid reed.

Huge waves like hungry wolves
Leap at the groaning headlands,
And stumbling through the forest frost
A starved stag sinks and shudders.

Nothing moves in the numbed marshes
Where captive in the bleak, blue ice,
All withered in the murderous weather
The sedge is black and gangrened.

THREE POEMS FROM THE WELSH OF ELWYN EVANS

(From ' Amser a Lle,' Gwasg Gomer, 1975)

JEWESS (IDDEWES)

BEHOLD the lovely Jewish girl
With ripening breasts that swell,
As if they wait the gentle maid's
Blessed motherhood in Israel.

SOLDIER (MILWR)

FAR from home, midst barren sands, an English
Friend I loved lies in the desert's keeping :
O brave, famed Arab of the burnished blade
Respect the small grave where he's sleeping.

ROMANCE (RHAMANT)

AFTER reading vivid novels of the Orient,
And tired of Wales which seemed so staid and sad,
I longed to seek for similar romances
In Cairo or Baghdad.

I'm in Baghdad, and I have been in Cairo
For just one unforgettable hour :
There was a tram-stop near the Pyramids,
The Nile stank like a sewer :
A factory makes pop beside the Tigris ?
Romance where *do* you flower ?

Our pathways crossed like fleeting picture postcards,
And here I grieve, and that's to say the least,
To know romance has blossomed in my homeland
And I'm in the Middle East !

O the magic lingering for me in the place-names,
The names I used to laugh at now and then,
Sketty, Cwmtwrch and Splott and Bagillt,
With Mumbles and Rhydyfen :
And now I'd give my all to spend the daylong
On the platform at Afonwen.

WRTH LAN Y MÔR

AR drothwy'r hwyr, mi welais gyda'r nos
Y sêr yn dyrfa ddistaw, deg uwchben
Yn nesu at ei gilydd dros y rhos,
A'r môr yn darian ddur o dan y nen :
Ac yna, gwylan unig ar ei hynt
Ddiymdrech yn noswylio dros y dŵr
Ar adain gref tuag adref, draw i'w thŵr
Tu hwnt i bell drigfannau cudd y gwynt.

A minnau'n gaeth wrth ddaear, isel nyth,
Heb ddringo i gwmni'r sêr neu'r creigiau glân,
Heb adain i ymgodi yno byth
Ond adain wan, aflonydd, fer fy nghân.

SAITH PENNILL O RUBAIYAT OMAR KHAYYAM

(Trosiad Saesneg Edward FitzGerald)

Bu rhai'n hwsmona ffrwyth yr euraid rawn
A rhai'n ei chwalu i'r gwyntoedd megis gwawn.
Ni thry neb hwy i'r un goludog bridd
A disgwyl cael o'u llwch gynhaeaf llawn.

Yn ifanc, minnau fûm o ddydd i ddydd
Yn eiddgar wrando'r saint a'r doethion sydd
Yn dadlau amgylch ogylch ; ond mi drois
Drwy'r drws yn ôl heb ronyn mwy o ffydd.

Hoff lyfyr cerdd dan gysgod cangen fry,
Fflasg win a thorth, a'th felys gwmni di
Yn swynol ganu yn yr anial dir
A'r holl anialwch yw fy nefoedd i !

Pa ddiben yw ailadrodd sut mae gwedd
Yn oriau chwim yn cludo'r dydd i'r bedd :
Mae fory yn y groth, a ddoe ar goll
Dewch, yfwch os yw heddiw'n hapus wledd !

Mae'r bys di-baid sydd yn cofnodi'n llawn
Yn brysur, nos a bore a phrynhawn,
Ac ofer ceisio golchi gair i ffwrdd
Drwy daer dduwioldeb, dagrau hallt na dawn.

Tyrd, llanw'r cwpan, O f'anwylyd cu
I chwalu gofid doe, a'r ofn o'n tu—
Yfory ? byddaf innau fory, siawns,
Fy hun gyda'r canrifoedd maith a fu.

Mae rhai fu'n annwyl inni, teg eu llun,
Ffrwyth graslon gwinllan amser, bob yr un,
Na chawsant fwy na blasu haf-win byw
Cyn cilio'n ddistaw i lonyddwch hun.

LLYN Y BALA

(*Nos Galan Gaeaf*)

Dros lyn y Bala cwyna'r gwynt
A'r gorsiar fach ar ben ei hynt
Yn llefain drwy ogofau'r nos :
Mae'r goedwig fain ar fin y rhos
Yn clywed lleisiau, chwithig, pell,
A llwyd gysgodion bedd a chell
Yn llercian rhwng llechweddau'r bryn . . .

Ond pwy wyf i, yn gwrando'n syn
Mewn dyrys ofn, i blymio'n siŵr
Dychryndod Aran ar ei thŵr
Yn crynu fel rhyw ddeilen wan ?
Digon yw dirnad unsain dŵr
Yn torri'n riddfan tua'r lan :
Na ddeil marwolion fwy na hyn
O hen anhunedd hir y llyn.

DEO GRATIAS

(Festival of Wales Prize Hymn, 1958. Set to music by E. T. Davies)

TODAY in gratitude we stand
To thank thee in these festal hours
For all thy blessings on our land,
This precious heritage of ours.

We thank thee for the brave who fought
To make us free in darker days,
And those who preached and prayed, and taught
Us music, poetry, art, and praise.

For those who saved our mother-tongue,
And men whose wisdom lit the way
For those whose skills have made us strong
And fruitful in this newer day.

Inspire our scientists who move
Within the mysteries of Thy might,
And grant them vision, faith and love
That each new gift be used aright.

We thank thee, Lord, for glimpses yet
Of noble eras still to be,
But guard us, lest we should forget
In mortal pride, to honour Thee.

In mercy let our children see
The banners of that dawn unfurled
When men, from want and fear set free,
Shall march as brothers through the world.

DEO GRATIAS

(Emyn Arobryn Gŵyl Cymru)

DIOLCHWN heddiw nefol Dad,
Yn oriau llawen gŵyl a gwledd,
Am holl fendithion hael ein gwlad
A'r etifeddiaeth deg a fedd.

Diolchwn am y dewrion roes
Eu rhodd o ryddid yn ein cur :
Am efengylwyr, dysgwyr moes,
Cerddorion, beirdd a chrefftwyr pur.

Am geidwaid cedyrn ein hoff iaith,
A'r rhai fu'n ddoeth yng ngrym eu ffydd
I'n tywys drwy drofeydd y daith
Hyd ffrwythlon fro ein newydd ddydd.

O dyro i'n gwyddonwyr sydd
Ar ymchwil yn Dy ddirgel dir
Y weledigaeth fawr a fydd
Yn arwain pawb i'r golau gwir.

Diolchwn, Iôr, am drem mor lân
Ar gyfnod gwell, heddychlon draw ;
Ond cadw ni, wrth deithio 'mlaen,
Rhag ymffrost gwag heb nerth Dy law.

O gad i'n plant groesawu'r dydd
Pan ddaw'r cenhedloedd yn un fryd,
O rwymau ofn ac eisiau'n rhydd,
I fyw fel brodyr drwy'r holl fyd.

GARDEN INTERLUDE

(For Scotty and Peg)

I RUMBLED a ghost in my garden,
He must have come up on my spade,
He'd served at the siege of Acre, he said,
In some tough Anglo-Norman brigade.

"Well, welcome," I said, "but please tell me
As I'm weak on the Third Crusade,
What things were like, and your wages,
Though I guess those were often unpaid."

"Oh no !" he replied, "them came pronto,
Just a penny a day we was paid,
And they chucked in an extra half-penny
Per week for my armourer's braid.

The heat there was hellish and awful,
Gawd knows how we scuttled for shade,
You couldn't tell beer from the water,
And we never had no lemonade.

King Richard, he coughed up a bonus
For us lads in his special brigade,
So we landed home happy and merry
At the end of that flamin' Crusade."

"A bonus," I echoed in sorrow,
"You've surfaced too soon, I'm afraid,
The tax-men will nab you for bonus,
And there's VAT overdue on your braid."

"Gorblimey," he muttered, "Gorblimey,
Than I reckon I ought to have stayed,
They can whistle for tax on my bonus,
And I won't pay a bean on my braid.

It's whispered down under, them Arabs
Are twisting you hard for their trade,
Just give us the nod, we'll be ready
To trip back again on parade."

I replied, "Since the deserts spout riches,
They're doing us down for their oil,
Don't worry, we'll manage like you did,
You're better off deep in the soil."

"Riches," he gasped in amazement,
"From oil in them heathenish lands,
Gorblimey, now who would have thought it
When we marched through them perishin' sands.

Well, thanks for your tip, I'll buzz off then,"
He said, looking sad and dismayed,
"Please call me when business looks brighter,
Let's hope it won't long be delayed."

Then he waved me goodbye and went under
And I patted him in with my spade :
So now they can't biff him for bonus,
Or catch him for VAT on his braid.